Henri
Matisse

By Roger Benjamin

RIZZOLI ART SERIES
Series Editor: Norma Broude

Henri
Matisse
(1869–1954)

The Body in Decoration[1]

As the fifth decade since Matisse's death draws near, interest in his work, as measured by volumes of publications and exhibitions large and small, continues to spiral. Yet research on Matisse does not match the intellectual interest and diversity of method generated by his contemporary Pablo Picasso. The remote personality and mostly proper private life of Matisse has discouraged the biographers and psychobiographers who cluster around the Spaniard.[2] The inscrutable nature of Matisse's political ideas and his limited contact with broader radical culture has meant that social contextualizations of his work have been slow in appearing.[3] However, the fact that Matisse was a cogent writer and commentator on his art, in a way that Picasso was not, has given rise to studies of his texts and their theoretical context that have lately taken a post-structuralist turn.[4] Feminists have begun to realize the potential for critique.[5] But to this day the dominant approach to the study of Matisse has been a formalist one, either as critical interpretation or as history of style.[6]

It has been suggested that the persistence of the formalist understanding of Matisse's achievement relates to his own position as one of the most successful propagators of high formalist art.[7] Matisse's 1908 "Notes of a Painter" probably offer the most influential model of art-making in the first half of this century. The "Notes" argue that the goal of art is expression and seemingly propose that manipulation of the painterly means within the confines of the canvas in itself provides sufficient meaning to the activity of art-making.[8] Matisse's paintings seem to vindicate this approach and to richly repay those formalist assessments that the artist helped to propagate.

Today, Matisse's art escapes the closure of such a limited system of understanding, and the symbol of that escape is the decorative. Decoration, in the pejorative sense of that which is superficial, was described by the critic Clement Greenberg (defender of American Abstract Expressionist art) as "the specter that haunts modernist painting." For Greenberg, too close an association of painting with the decorative arts could trivialize the former; only Matisse could "assimilate to easel painting devices that used to seem irredeemably decorative" and still produce highly successful pictures.[9] Skepticism about the value of Matisse's art grew in the late 1960s: the decorative component in his work seemed to Conceptual artists proof of a bourgeois hedonism and lack of intellectual substance.

More recent developments in postmodernism have vindicated Matisse in at least two ways. First, it now appears that the anxiety of formalist critics with the decorative was really anxiety about popular culture, about a threat to the pristine elevation of high art posed by mass-produced and commercialized design. The amenability of Matisse's art to such domains is evident in visual culture today: his painted work is widely diffused in posters, in postcards, even in the witticisms of the appropriation artist. Owing to the adaptability of the process of designing by flat colored shapes that Matisse introduced in the 1940s, his paper cutouts (plates 13 and 14) print easily onto the surfaces of T-shirts, inform the look of designer fabrics and album covers, and even find echoes in postmodern furniture and architecture.

Second, decoration, pattern-making, a concern with ornament, and the employment of unorthodox materials have been reclaimed for art-making by the women's movement since the 1970s. Anonymous women's decorative work has been given positive value, and various forms of popular expression recuperated as having valuable cultural meaning for their primarily female practitioners.[10] The supposed "feminine" element had long played a tacit role in downgrading the value of the decorative arts, as well as paintings that appeared "decorative" in effect. But Matisse, it is important to note, had none of the contempt for the decorative that later male formalists evinced. Rather, he embraced it in his statements: "The decorative is an extremely precious thing for a work of art. It is an essential quality. It is not pejorative to say that an artist's paintings are decorative."[11]

In another way however, the development of Matisse's new aesthetic of the decorative was made at the expense of women—not women as producers of art, but women as subjects, as the bodies that figure in the painter's decorative canvases. In Matisse's work, the human body becomes a decorative motif thrown freely into the pictorial arena. Liberating the decorative sense of the body did not, in Matisse's hands, mean abandoning its potential as a symbol. As with movements of the figure on the modern dance stage, Matisse's work could propose a new consciousness of the body as an animal and gestural entity. But Matisse's way of doing this nevertheless meant perpetuating traditional social inequities between men and women.

The body had long been the prime subject in the humanist ideology of painting, which aimed to imitate worthy human actions so as morally to uplift the viewer. When the young Matisse joined the studio of Gustave Moreau at the Ecole des Beaux-Arts in Paris in 1891, representing the human figure was still the key institution of the academic system. The body was copied from plaster casts of antique statues, drawn from life before professional models, and rendered in oils as *académies*—models studied as exercises in techniques of sketching-in, modeling, and finishing. The twenty-two-year-old Matisse had the necessary education (in grammar school and legal studies) to pursue fruitfully the highest level of academic work: figure paintings of literary or historical themes. Yet Matisse's robustly positivist disposition and interest in the independent art of the Impressionists meant that his figure paintings quickly broke free from the impeccable idealized physiques of academic nudes, as well as from their literary thematics.

Figures begun as *académies* became in themselves sufficient to constitute the work of making a picture. Thus, in

1900 the focus of Matisse's activity and that of his colleagues was the standing, naked body, most usually that of a woman. *Nude Study in Blue* (plate 1) is a characteristic presentation of this primal scene of figure painting: the record of a group of young men together sharing the sight of a female nude. The woman's gesture of modesty in response to the frontal posture of her body encodes the gendered relation between the male painter and female model: the male gaze issues a threat of possession, sexual and aesthetic, upon the coerced body of the model. A formalist, by ignoring the power relations between artist and model, would see the woman's body as an unproblematic subject for experiments in pictorial style. From a feminist perspective, however, the process might constitute an elaborate depersonalization of women,[12] in which the female body is reduced to a "territory across which men artists claim their modernity and compete for leadership of the avant-garde."[13]

The painter with whom Matisse "competed" in his paintings around 1900 was Paul Cézanne, the reclusive Post-Impressionist whose new mode of structuring pictorial space galvanized Matisse. In Cézanne's *Bathers* series (one of which Matisse had purchased), imagined male and female bodies move freely in a landscape setting. Cézanne rendered them with a technical awkwardness partly due to his refusal to use live models. By contrast, Matisse's painting of the nude throughout his career was usually closely dependent on specifically observed, individual female models. His *Nude Study in Blue* thus revises Cézanne in that its abbreviations and distortions—effects of a kind that came to be called decorative—are the product of the strict study of a specific model. The mental life of this figure is not a focus of the painting: according to an eyewitness, Matisse in 1900 was instead preoccupied with the "animal mechanics" of the body, using a plumbline and measurements to achieve a "beautiful plastic power."[14]

The next encounter in Matisse's assimilation of avant-garde painting is recorded in *Open Window at Collioure* of 1905 (plate 3), which with its vivid complementary colors and staccato texture bears the trace of his previous year's painting in the Pointillist style of Paul Signac and Georges Seurat. Yet *Open Window* is even more emblematic of the art of the Fauves, the group of so-called "Wild Beasts" who, led by Matisse and André Derain, exhibited from 1905 to 1908 at the newly instituted annual exhibition of progressive art, the Salon d'Automne.

Today the *Open Window* seems a more controlled experiment than the majority of Fauve canvases. In formal terms, its design offers a play upon the traditional understanding of a picture as window-on-the-world: framed view appears within framed view, rehearsing the compositional bracketing by which a painter delimits a scene for intense aesthetic analysis. The picture is activated by colors that, symptomatically for Fauve art, cannot be a record of what was observed: Matisse's model could not have had an intensity of color and light inside the room equal to that of the sunlit outside world. Colored relations within the picture refer, above all, back to each other—the blue of the boats is identical with that in the foreground shadows; the invented puce of one wall answers, in a compositional sense, the green of the other.

Such features conform to the concept of a picture as a self-referring construction that was developing within high modernist art at the beginning of the twentieth century:

1. *Joy of Life*. 1905–1906. Oil on canvas, 68½ x 93¾".
Photograph ©1992 The Barnes Foundation, Merion Station, Pennsylvania

although the artist sought to render what was given to his sensations, the "rights" of the developing picture took precedence. As Matisse wrote in "Notes of a Painter": "There is an impelling proportion of tones that may lead me to change the shape of a figure or to transform my composition. . . . I cannot copy nature in a servile way, I am forced to interpret nature and submit it to the spirit of the picture." The complex texture of brushwork in *Open Window* brings out this transformative process: from smoothly brushed planes to interweaving filigree, Matisse's paint strokes recode what he sees in patterns that also correspond to the dialects of contemporary art: a Van Gogh idiom for the boats' masts, Signac strokes for the water, Gauguinesque planes for the walls.

The subject of such a picture, or of Matisse's *Joy of Life* (fig. 1) of the following year, can be placed within the purview of the decorative. At the turn of the century the term "decorative painting" referred first of all to large-scale mural pictures of a kind designed for specific installations. Their subjects usually accorded with the function of the room they decorated, be they allegories of civic duty for town halls or country scenes for private dining rooms. This "decorum," or sense of appropriateness, also affected easel painting: in *Open Window* the cheery spectacle of fishing-boats bobbing in a sunny Mediterranean harbor seems appropriate to the desire of middle-class urban dwellers for a symbol of escape to zones altogether apart from the city. But in 1905 the middle-class viewer was in fact not yet amenable to such seduction—this painting was one of the most reviled for its experimental extravagance when it was exhibited at the Salon d'Automne in Paris.

The *Joy of Life* corresponded even more closely with ideas Matisse expressed in his "Notes" on the goal of his art as recreational therapy for the bourgeois "mental worker." The theme is frankly utopian: it proposes free love among figures reclining upon the grass and partaking of dance and informal music as another vision of ideal existence appropriate for the adornment of the mundane urban interior. Certain visual parameters of the work also correspond to the decorative conception: a scale large enough to cover a wall, layers of thin but bright color, and design by a series of planes that delimit the figural motif according to classical conventions of composition.

It is in the *Joy of Life* that the role of the body as the paradigmatic motif in Matisse's decorative painting is first

2. *Decorative Figure.* 1908. Bronze, 28¹/₁₆ x 20 x 12". Hirshhorn Museum and Sculpture Garden, Smithsonian Institution. Gift of Joseph H. Hirshhorn, 1966

essayed. The ring of dancers is later expanded in the great decors of 1910 (plate 6) and 1930, while the central reclining figure recurs in works from the *Blue Nude* of 1906–1907 (plate 4) to the *Pink Nude* (plate 11) of 1935. In formal terms, one could say the hallmark of this decorative paradigm of the body is an arrangement of limbs that produces an emphatic play of axes held together by the continuous curved lines described by the contours of the (usually) female body. In particular, it is the curved silhouettes that Matisse produced in the hips, waists, and breasts of female bodies that unite the parts of the picture within an overall arabesque conception of the figure.

However, such a view ignores Matisse's use of the body to encode explicit eroticism. Late in life the artist admitted of his models (somewhat elliptically given the intimate relationship he had with some of them, in particular Mme. Matisse): "The emotional interest aroused in me by them does not appear particularly in the representation of their bodies, but often rather in the lines or the special values distributed over the whole canvas. . . . It is perhaps sublimated sensual pleasure, which may not yet be perceived by everyone."[15]

Such a sexual dynamic was already present in the *Blue Nude*, the work that succeeded in distancing the avant-gardist Matisse from any public consensus about the appearance of the female body. The two official salons in Paris were still cluttered with nudes painted according to academic norms for correct drawing and meticulous finish. At the Salon d'Automne, more experimental paintings of the female nude had come under the attack of conservatives for their "methodical disgrace of the flesh," wherein women were painted with "a strange misogyny which sought to render them repellent."[16] Matisse was considered a prime offender: even former supporters like Louis Vauxcelles found the new aesthetic too violently remote from academic norms, describing the *Blue Nude* as an "ugly nude woman" rendered in "rudimentary drawing" and "crude coloring." Vauxcelles even sensed an ambivalence in the figure's gender, calling it a "mannish nymph."[17] A "feminine" nude was supposed to be svelte and smooth in her flesh, while Matisse's was large-boned, muscular, and wore her hair

short. The energized pose of the figure could be perceived as a sexual aggressiveness uncomfortable to the male critic. Only the situation of the figure might neutralize that threat: the *Blue Nude* is shown in a faraway tropical decor, as an odalisque by an oasis (the subtitle is *Souvenir of Biskra*, after the North African town Matisse visited in 1906).

In sculpted figures Matisse could provide no such alibi for experiment: his significantly titled *Decorative Figure* (fig. 2) had to succeed as pure body sufficient unto itself. An emphatic working of the clay surface into a coruscated skin, an orchestration of curves so determining that a foot disappears into the sculpture's base: such elements are complemented by a quizzical sense of psychic presence in the oversize head, which is a portrait of Mme. Matisse. The arabesque principles of twisting axes and contrapposto betray Matisse's interest in Renaissance sculpture in the tradition of Michelangelo or the small bronzes of Giovanni da Bologna.[18] In the galleries of the Louvre a modernist like Matisse would have been less interested in the literary rationale of such bronzes—miniature versions of heroic figures—than in the potential inherent in their small scale and decorative function. For the post-symbolist Matisse, weaned on readings of Baudelaire, Delacroix, and Mallarmé, such suggestive imprecision of meaning was desirable. As he wrote in his "Notes" of Giotto's frescoes in Padua: "I do not trouble myself to recognize which scene of the Life of Christ I have before me, but I immediately understand the sentiment emerging from it, for it is in the lines, the composition, the color."

The first decorative project in which Matisse could address the ambitious scale of Giotto's frescoes was in the canvas panels *Dance* (plate 6) and *Music*, commissioned by the Russian magnate Sergei N. Shchukin to decorate his Moscow mansion. This project marks Matisse's accession, in his forty-second year, to the elite of painters who earned large sums of money working to commission (his pictorial radicalism however excluded Matisse from any decoration of public buildings). Commentators have often remarked on the unparalleled reduction of means evident in these works. His colleague Pierre Bonnard, on questioning the lack of modeling evident in *Dance*, was given the reply, "What's the use complicating my problem?"[19] In formalist terms, the procedure results in an intensification of energy produced by the contrast of colored zones, such that the space surrounding the figures can be experienced as itself proposing a field of disembodied color, of pure opticality; effectively these panels are the ancestors of all subsequent "color-field" painting.

The circle of giant dancers is an iconographical motif of great resonance, evoking pictorial memories ranging from figures decorating prehistoric rock galleries to the classicizing dancers of the Old Masters Poussin or Ingres. Part of this ubiquity of reference is the result of Matisse's modernist universalization—the figures are highly generalized, to the point that their gender is apparently indeterminate. Yet upon closer inspection, the nakedness of the generic bodies in the panels breaks down into gendered components: the whirling figures in *Dance* appear to be women, while those passive, absorbed figures making music in the other picture are men (we know Matisse was obliged to paint out the genitals at the request of his patron, who feared a scandal). In that sense women are reduced to pure physicality, to acts of nature, while men are reflective, producers of culture: the women dance to the men's tune. The parallelism thus reproduces the relationship between Matisse and his models. Matisse may have challenged the role of the figure in painting, but in doing so he reaffirmed current stereotypes of gender.

The complexity of Matisse's art, with its links to Western concepts of self-expression, to the "primitive" arts of Africa, and to Oriental traditions of decoration is embodied in the pronounced arabesque element in *Dance*. In the nineteenth century the term "arabesque" referred, in Western pictorial and decorative arts, to a kind of flat pattern comprising plant motifs that reminded admirers of the patterns of Islamic art. The term could also be used to describe any more general instance of a turning, writhing movement in the arts.

As a device rich in metaphoric content, the arabesque was by no means tied to the representation of figures alone. The arabesque presumably owes its resonance to its relation to the human form; when that specific form is absent, the aura of significance attached to the arabesque may be maintained by other means.[20] The organic nature of the motif ensures that it endows more strictly decorative works with meaning. So in Islamic decorative art, abstract, repeating motifs based on the movements of plants, or elements of calligraphic Kufic script might come to take up the function of the figure in the work of art. Matisse, who had for years been actively interested in Persian and other forms of Islamic art, was capable of adapting and transforming such a lesson in such compositions as his *Interior with Eggplants* (plate 7).

Here the paisley motifs at the heart of the picture replace in size and cursive visual interest an absent figure group. The work appears as a play of decorated surfaces, like a collage on a grand scale. In Persian miniature art much of the visual interest for Western audiences derives from the juxtaposing of intensely patterned and colored surfaces. The five-pointed purple flower motif that Matisse strews across *Interior with Eggplants* probably alludes to such decoration.[21] The motif defies rational space by having the same value in dark or bright areas of the room. Because it is not positioned in perspective, the motif's role is decorative, not representational.

Matisse's art was thus artificial—concerned with interpreting elements in a prearranged universe. Yet he also had a positivist side, which meant that, like many of his peers in the generation after the Impressionists, Matisse actively sought new sensations by varying his physical environment. This is evident in his trips to Brittany in the late 1890s, to St. Tropez and Collioure in 1904–1906, and Algeria, Italy, and Spain as the *succès de scandale* of Fauvism began from 1906 to translate into increased earnings. Only in Morocco in the winters of 1911 and 1912 did Matisse undertake a full range of subjects: interiors, landscapes, portraits, and figure paintings of local types. Thus Matisse continued the tradition of French Orientalist painters for whom contact with the culturally or geographically alien was sought as a stimulus to painting. The exotic could be provided in abundance by travel to the French colonies in North Africa, Indochina, or Polynesia.

A painting such as *Zorah on the Terrace* (plate 8) records a spectacle of the exotic: a corner of brilliant African sun-

3. *The Plumed Hat*. 1919. Pencil on paper, 20⅞ x 14⅜". ©The Detroit Institute of Arts. Bequest of John S. Newberry

light on the casbah terrace, a dark-skinned girl who kneels smiling before Matisse, and the colorism of a traditional costume he had her don for the occasion. These things are interpreted with the aesthetic elation of the itinerant artist in colonial Tangier, but have little to do with the difficult situation of his model considered either personally (she was about to become a prostitute) or as a representative of her country (recently annexed as a French protectorate).[22] Although an artist of liberal conscience, Matisse had no interest whatever in social realism. Instead he painted what he would later call a "decorative portrait," working outwards from the sitter and the blue wash of the casbah walls to construct an airy fantasy of painterliness in which Zorah is set like a glowing jewel, almost as if the timeless world of the Arabian Nights, before Western intervention, might still exist.

Works like *Zorah* or *The Yellow Curtain* (plate 9) of 1914 record, on a stylistic level, Matisse's response to the breakup of perspectival representation introduced by Cubist painting. In point of abstraction and for the sheer hermeticism of its subject, *The Yellow Curtain* concedes very little to the Cubists. Longer than any of his peers during the years of World War I (he was forty-five at its outbreak and not accepted for military service), Matisse maintained his commitment to such experimentation. But when Matisse's "return to order" came in the closing years of the war, it came with a vengeance. There has been debate as to whether the many paintings Matisse produced during the first Nice period (1917–1930), during which he moved from Paris to live in the Mediterranean city, represent not only an abandonment of the experimentation linked by later twentieth-century critics with the program of modernist art, but also a net loss in "quality."[23]

Matisse's about-face, his return to correct perspective and a largely normative palette, his refusal of his habitual distortion and development of a feathery late-Impressionist brush style (he was close to Renoir in these years), marks his reabsorption into the more conventional stream of postwar School of Paris painting. Matisse was definitely a participant in the 1920s "return to order," with its revivals of neo-classical styles and crisply realist drawing in the hands of such artists as André Derain, Pablo Picasso, and Gino Severini. Matisse should be linked with that broad movement and the cultural and political reasons that have been adduced for its appearance.[24]

The easy rhythm of the wrist that could bring structural weakness to Matisse's canvases of this time resulted, in many of his drawings and lithographs, in a mellifluous play of precisely orchestrated arabesques (see *The Plumed Hat*, fig. 3). Matisse's drawing, which in the years 1906–1914 had initiated a style of radical simplification, of resuming appearances in a minimum number of nervous, edgy traits, from the 1920s on offered that simplification in a svelte autography of taut yet languorous line. For some, the voluptuousness of this draftsmanship is part of Matisse's appeal; it may be seen as a translation of the erotic relation between artist and model (for example, the sitter for *Large Blue Dress and Mimosas* [plate 12] was Mme. Lydia Delektorskaya, Matisse's secretary, model, and lover).

Such an eroticization is evident in the decorative canvases of Matisse's odalisques, European models who performed an elaborate masquerade at the artist's behest amongst the Orientalist props of his Nice studio. Matisse claimed he painted these odalisques "in order to do nudes. . . . And then, because I know that they exist. I was in Morocco. I have seen them."[25] No amount of earlier "authentic" experience in the touristic environment of Tangiers can however disguise the extreme artifice of these pictures. The decorative element in them consists in a piling-up of ornamented cloths, curtains, inlaid tables, and Persian screens into a phantasmagoria of patterned surfaces. A work like *Odalisque in Red Trousers* (plate 10) presents a decor depicted with considerable detail and finesse of touch. The body of the woman is set out in skillfully managed foreshortening, the torso being painted with a solidity that betrays Matisse's continuing admiration for Courbet. It is symptomatic that this most technically conservative of Matisse's canvases, replete with fantasized colonial thematics, should have been the first canvas since the artist's Fauve days to be acquired by the French national collections.[26]

In his work after his 1930 trip to Tahiti and the United States, beginning with the great mural commissioned for the Barnes Foundation in Merion, Pennsylvania, Matisse returned to an investigation of the body that went beyond ornament through the use of costume. Certain works are decorative in the full Matissean sense of making free with human anatomy in order to better serve the composition. The result, in a work such as *Pink Nude* of 1935 (plate 11), is a new sense of physicality: a painting with the same modest dimensions as the *Odalisque in Red Trousers*, the *Pink Nude* nevertheless develops a quite different sense of spatial and corporeal expansiveness. The gulf between the two conceptions indicates the extent to which Matisse, against all expectations (he was sixty in 1929, an age at which certain Parisian critics regarded him as "washed up"[27]), was able to reinvigorate the experimental aspect of his art in the last two decades of his life.

Matisse's late cutouts are one of his most significant contributions to twentieth-century visual culture. The first of them appeared to help address the problem of presenting the body in decoration: Matisse used colored paper in maquettes for his giant arched mural of the *Dance*, painted in

4. *The Parakeet and the Mermaid.* 1952. Gouache cutout pasted on paper, 132¹¹/₁₆ x 304³/₈". The Stedelijk Museum, Amsterdam

1932 for the central hall of the Barnes Foundation. Extrapolating from the way the summary figures of the 1910 *Dance* were already optically detached from their environment, Matisse used cutout sheets of paper to construct a jigsaw of interlocking planes with the contours of human bodies. The applications of the technique were many: from establishing designs for the Barnes paintings or the Vence Chapel stained-glass windows in the South of France to providing the images for the silkscreened book *Jazz* (plate 13) to the use of cut paper attached to walls in the great environmental decorations of the early 1950s (plate 14).

The very large cutouts dialogue in scale and ambition with mural decorations of a kind executed on public commission in Matisse's youth by artists like Puvis de Chavannes (an official but progressive artist admired by Matisse's generation). Yet the best of the cutouts turned Matisse's ideas on the restorative function of decorative art back onto his private self: they were set up to provide solace for the aged artist, largely bedridden in his Nice apartment after a life-threatening operation in 1941. So the forty-five-foot *Swimming Pool* (plate 14) initially decorated the four walls of Matisse's dining room, like a modern-day version of a Renaissance prince's cabinet. The artist said of it: "I have always adored the sea, and now that I can no longer go for a swim, I have surrounded myself with it."[28] Elements in blue paper work their way in and around a pictorial field—the swimming pool—defined by a white band across burlap panels. The color blue functions simultaneously as the fantasized bodies of swimmers cavorting and exercising in the water, and then, by switching through the silhouette from figure to ground, the blue paper becomes water itself, splashed up into shreds of light and color. As a solution to the question of the body in decoration, the *Swimming Pool* dehierarchizes the figure, on the one hand assimilating it to abstract aquatic shapes, on the other by reifying the "background" so that the figure dissolves into the overall decorative scheme, just as a swimmer submerges in the waters of a pool.

The absorption of the figure into decoration reaches its most extreme state in Matisse's *The Parakeet and the Mermaid* (fig. 4), which replaces *Swimming Pool*'s sense of narrative with patterned uniformity. Initially wrapped around two walls of his Nice studio, this work is the closest Matisse came to producing an "all-over" composition: one that had neither center nor hard edges that affected the layout of contained elements. In presenting his endless garden, at once marine and arboreal (the cutout leaves could be both fronds of kelp or tropical foliage), Matisse plays upon the strict patterns of machine-made decorations, such as floral wallpaper or printed cloth. Whereas the principle of mass-produced decoration is the repetition of interlocking motifs strung across a hidden grid structure, the patterns produced in *The Parakeet and the Mermaid* by Matisse and his assistants are based upon a judgement of the eye. They toy with repetition and the grid, defeating regularity at every turn. Hence they proclaim the handmade character of this decoration: it is a one-off creation, a work of luxury that defines itself as art precisely in its ironic distance from the mechanical and the mass-produced. Yet the popular arts in our time have enthusiastically appropriated this expansive pastiche of their own appearance.

Matisse stands out among the key practitioners of high modernist art for his comprehension of the value of decoration. His own pressing need for the decorative, evident both in his making cutouts and his life-long collecting of ornamental objects and fabrics, indicates the extent to which Matisse could equate the activity of "losing oneself" in the patterns of decorative art with that of "finding oneself" in a picture. Personal identity may turn upon any kind of image, irrespective of its origin; for such insights Matisse commands our interest long after the narrow exclusions of mid–twentieth-century art criticism have fallen away.

NOTES

1. Thanks are due to David Bennett, Hélène Hourmat, Louise Marshall, and Chris McAuliffe for help in preparing this volume.
2. See the revealing portrait in Jane Simone Bussy, "A Great Man," *Burlington Magazine*, 128 (February 1986), pp. 80–84.
3. E.g. Kenneth E. Silver, *Esprit de Corps* (Princeton: Princeton University Press, 1989).
4. See Benjamin, 1987, on the texts and Yve-Alain Bois, "*Matisse and 'Arche-Drawing,'*" in *Painting as Model* (Cambridge: MIT Press, 1990), pp. 3–63.
5. E.g. Marilyn L. Board, "Constructing Myths and Ideologies in Matisse's Odalisques," *Genders*, 5 (July 1989), pp. 21–49.
6. The writings of Elderfield and Flam are variants on this approach.
7. See James D. Herbert, "Matisse without History" (rev. of Schneider, 1984, and Flam, 1986), *Art History*, 11 (June 1988), pp. 297–302.
8. Henri Matisse, "Notes d'un Peintre," *Grande Revue*, 52 (December 25, 1908), trans. Flam, 1973, pp. 35–40.
9. Clement Greenberg, *Art and Culture* (Boston: Beacon Books, 1961), p. 148, 200.
10. See Norma Broude, "Miriam Schapiro and 'Femmage,'" *Feminism and Art History*, eds. N. Broude and M. Garrard (New York: Harper and Row, 1982), and Rozsika Parker, *The Subversive Stitch* (London: Women's Press, 1984).
11. Léon Degand, "Matisse à Paris," *Les Lettres Françaises*, 76 (October 6, 1945).
12. See Rosemary Betterton, "How Do Women Look? The Nudes of Suzanne Valadon," *Looking On*, ed. R. Betterton (London: Pandora, 1987), pp. 217–234.
13. Griselda Pollock, *Vision and Difference* (London: Routledge, 1988), p. 54.
14. Jean Puy, "Souvenirs," *Le Point*, 21 (July 1939), p. 22.
15. Henri Matisse, "Notes of a Painter on His Drawing" (1939), Flam, 1973, p. 82.
16. Camille Mauclair, "La Crise de la laideur en peinture," *Les Trois Crises de la peinture actuelle* (Paris: Fasquelle, 1906), pp. 296–297.
17. Louis Vauxcelles, "Le Salon des Indépendants," *Gil Blas* (March 20, 1907).
18. See Roger Benjamin, "L'Arabesque dans la modernité: Henri Matisse sculpteur," *De Matisse à aujourd'hui: la sculpture du XXe siècle* (Calais: Association des Conservateurs des Musées du Nord-Pas-de-Calais, 1992), pp. 15–25.
19. Henri Matisse, quoted in Barr, 1951, p. 138.
20. See Roger Benjamin, "The Decorative Landscape and the Arabesque of Observation," forthcoming in *The Art Bulletin*.
21. See Dominique Fourcade, "Rêver à trois aubergines. . . .," *Critique*, 324 (May 1974), pp. 467–489.
22. See Roger Benjamin, "A Colonizing Esthetic? Matisse in Morocco," *Art in America*, 78 (November 1990), pp. 156–165, 211–213.
23. See Cowart and Fourcade, 1986, and Kenneth E. Silver, "Matisse's 'Retour à l'ordre,'" *Art in America*, 75 (June 1987), pp. 110–123, 167–169.
24. See Silver, 1987, and Benjamin H. D. Buchloh, "Figures of Authority, Ciphers of Regression," *October*, 16 (Spring 1981), pp. 39–68.
25. Matisse, "Statements to Tériade, 1929–1930," Flam, 1973, p. 59.
26. See Silver, 1987, p. 122.
27. E.g. Fritz Neugass, "Henri-Matisse," *L'Amour de l'Art*, 24, 106 (April 1930), p. 240.
28. Matisse to Mrs. Alfred Barr, cited in Elderfield, 1978, p. 30.

FURTHER READING

Barr, Alfred H., Jr. *Matisse, His Art and His Public*. New York: Museum of Modern Art, 1951.

Benjamin, Roger. *Matisse's "Notes of a Painter": Criticism, Theory and Context, 1891–1908*. Ann Arbor: UMI Research Press, 1987.

—————————. "Recovering Authors: The Modern Copy, Copy Exhibitions and Matisse." *Art History*, 12, 2 (June 1989), pp.176–201.

Cowart, Jack, and Dominique Fourcade. *Henri Matisse: The Early Years in Nice, 1916–1930*. Washington and New York: National Gallery of Art and Harry N. Abrams, 1986.

Cowart, Jack, Pierre Schneider, and John Elderfield. *Matisse in Morocco: The Paintings and Drawings, 1912–1913*. Washington: National Gallery of Art, 1990.

Elderfield, John. *The Cut-Outs of Henri Matisse*. New York: George Braziller, 1978.

Elsen, Albert E. *The Sculpture of Henri Matisse*. New York: Harry N. Abrams, 1972.

Flam, Jack, ed. *Matisse on Art*. Oxford: Phaidon, 1973.

—————————. *Matisse: The Man and His Art, 1869–1918*. Ithaca: Cornell University Press, 1986.

Freeman, Judi, Roger Benjamin, James D. Herbert, John Klein, and Alvin Martin. *The Fauve Landscape*. Los Angeles and New York: Los Angeles County Museum of Art and Abbeville Press, 1990.

Schneider, Pierre. *Matisse*. New York: Rizzoli, 1984.

First published in 1992 in the United States of America by Rizzoli International Publications, Inc.
300 Park Avenue South
New York, New York 10010

Copyright ©1992 Rizzoli International Publications, Inc.
Text copyright ©1992 Roger Benjamin·
©1992 Succession H. Matisse/ARS, N.Y.

Library of Congress Cataloging-in-Publication Data
Benjamin, Roger, 1957–
  Henri Matisse/by Roger Benjamin.
    p. cm. — (Rizzoli art series)
    Includes bibliographical references and index.
    ISBN 0-8478-1610-9
    1. Matisse, Henri, 1869–1954—Criticism and interpretation.
I. Matisse, Henri, 1869–1954 II. Title. III. Series.
ND553.M37B37   1992
759.4—dc20   92-15546
                                                               CIP

Series Editor: Norma Broude

Series designed by José Conde and Betty Lew/Rizzoli
Printed in Singapore
Fig. 2 photographed by Lee Stalsworth
Colorplate 3 photographed by Jim Strong
Colorplate 15 photographed by Philippe Migeat
Front cover: detail of colorplate 6

Index to Colorplates

1. *Nude Study in Blue*. 1899–1900.
One of a series of nudes standing in the studio in which the details of the model's facial features are sacrificed to the artist's desire for equal painterly weight in all parts of the canvas. The woman's body is thus put to work as an armature for the display of pictorial effects.

2. *Copy of "La Raie" by Chardin*.
1897–1902. Matisse supplemented his income as a student by selling copies of Louvre masterpieces to the state. This copy became an exercise in personal interpretation, "with Cézanne there behind it." That made a sale impossible, but helped to establish Matisse's fascination with rendering the interrelationship between objects in a still life.

3. *Open Window at Collioure*. 1905.
One of two Matisses reproduced in the magazine *L'Illustration*'s spread on the 1905 Salon d'Automne, where the paintings of the "Wild Beasts" created an uproar. A sympathetic critic wrote that Matisse was "going astray in passionate research, demanding of Pointillism more vibration, more luminosity. But the concern for form suffers."

4. *Blue Nude (Souvenir of Biskra)*.
1906–1907.
In 1908 Matisse wrote: "Suppose I want to paint a woman's body: first of all I imbue it with grace and charm, but I know that I must give something more. I will condense the meaning of this body by seeking its essential lines." The overpainting, erasures, and forceful outlining visible in *Blue Nude* are part of this intensification of the image of the body.

5. *Still Life with Fruit and Bronze*. 1910.
Matisse frequently used pieces of cloth with strong patterns as the unifying backdrop of a still life. Here a semi-tribal Persian rug provides a curved frame upon which the fruit, ceramics, and statuette (his 1908 sculpture *Group of Two Women*) seem suspended in space. The intense motifs and colors of the rug merge with other elements in the overall design.

6. *Dance*. 1910. In 1909 Matisse said of his decorations for Shchukin's staircase in Moscow: "As [the visitor] needs to make an effort, one must give him a feeling of lightness. My first panel represents the dance, that whirling round on the top of the hill." Matisse's energetic theme reflects the painting's location.

7. *Interior with Eggplants*. 1911.
The picture shows Matisse's studio at Collioure, with a revealing window opening onto the landscape at right. It was painted in the flat, crumbly medium of distemper, sometimes used for temporary decorations. The work originally had a painted border of flower motifs (removed after 1922), which heightened its pronounced decorative effect.

8. *Zorah on the Terrace*. 1912.
This work is part of the "Moroccan Triptych" Matisse painted for Ivan Morosov. *Zorah* and *The Casbah Gate* were painted inside the old Arab citadel of Tangiers. They are unusual in contemporary painting in presenting the picturesque Orientalist themes of costumed indigenous model and architecture in an experimental, abstract mode.

9. *The Yellow Curtain*. 1914–1915.
One of the most abstract of all Matisse's works; there is no certainty (beyond the red curtain at left and the green wall framing the window) about what is seen: is it a yellow hill with blue sky above and a pool below, or, as Matisse's daughter said, a blue glass canopy over the doorway below and yellow flowering bushes in the garden above?

10. *Odalisque in Red Trousers*. 1921.
When this work was bought by the Musée du Luxembourg in 1922, English critic Roger Fry hailed it thus: "The magical qualities of Henri-Matisse's color are universally recognized. . . . Almost alone Matisse seems able to retain freshness and delicacy while intensifying to the utmost point the resonance and purity of his local colors."

11. *Large Reclining Nude*, formerly *Pink Nude*. 1935.
This painting illustrates Matisse's long-established practice of obsessively painting, effacing with thinners, and repainting a canvas until he was satisfied. The *Pink Nude* started out as far more conventional in its perspectival rendition of the figure.

12. *Large Blue Dress and Mimosas*. 1937.
In his essay "Portraits" (1954), Matisse wrote: "The likeness of a portrait comes from the contrast which exists between the face of the model and other faces. . . . Each figure has its own rhythm and it is this rhythm which creates the likeness." Here the portrait of Lydia Delektorskaya in a ruffled gown is complemented by a probable profile of her pinned to the wall.

13. *Icarus*, from *Jazz*. 1943.
One of 20 illustrations for the book *Jazz* (1947) comprising gouache cutouts on themes of the circus, popular tales, and travel. Of the Greek hero Icarus, whose attempt to fly was defeated by the sun, Alfred Barr wrote, "His heart is reduced to a palpitating scarlet dot which scarcely animates his dangling limbs as he falls through deep blue infinity."

14. *Swimming Pool*. 1952.
A Surreal impulse was present in Matisse's transformation of the four walls of his Nice dining room into a swimming pool viewed from within. The subject, with its worship of physical culture and the refraction of naked, athletic bodies in blue water, was rediscovered a decade later by the artist David Hockney in California.

15. *Large Red Interior*. 1948.
This still life, created in the last year Matisse could practice oil painting, incorporates two contemporary works—a drawing in Chinese ink and *The Pineapple*—both dominating the composition. Including his own works in the signature red interior makes of Matisse's picture a kind of portrait of the self via external objects.

1. *Nude Study in Blue*. 1899–1900. Oil on canvas, 29 x 21".
Tate Gallery, London/Art Resource, New York

2. Copy of "La Raie" by Chardin. 1897–1902. Oil on canvas. 45 x 56".
Musée Matisse, Le Cateau-Cambrésis

3. *Open Window at Collioure*. 1905. Oil on canvas, 22 x 18".
From the Collection of Mrs. John Hay Whitney

4. *Blue Nude (Souvenir of Biskra)*. 1907. Oil on canvas, 36 x 55".
The Baltimore Museum of Art. The Cone Collection, formed by
Dr. Claribel Cone and Miss Etta Cone of Baltimore, Maryland. BMA 1950.228

5. *Still Life with Fruit and Bronze*. 1910. Oil on canvas, 35 x 45".
The Pushkin Fine Arts Museum, Moscow/Art Resource, New York

6. *Dance.* 1910. Oil on canvas, 102 x 153".
The Hermitage Museum, St. Petersburg/Art Resource, New York

7. *Interior with Eggplants*. 1911. Tempera and mixed techniques on canvas, 83 x 96".
Photograph Musée de Grenoble/André Morin

8. *Zorah on the Terrace.* 1912. Oil on canvas, 45 x 39".
The Pushkin Fine Arts Museum, Moscow/Art Resource, New York

9. *The Yellow Curtain*. 1914–1915. Oil on canvas, 52 x 38".
Private collection

10. *Odalisque in Red Trousers.* 1921. Oil on canvas, 25 x 35".
Photograph ©Musée National d'Art Moderne, Centre Georges Pompidou, Paris

11. *Large Reclining Nude*, formerly *Pink Nude*. 1935. Oil on canvas, 26 x 36".
The Baltimore Museum of Art. The Cone Collection, formed by
Dr. Claribel Cone and Miss Etta Cone of Baltimore, Maryland. BMA 1950.258

12. *Large Blue Dress and Mimosas.* 1937. Oil on canvas, 36 x 29".
©Philadelphia Museum of Art. Gift of Mrs. John Wintersteen

13. *Icarus*, from *Jazz* (Paris: Teriade), 1947. Pochoir, printed in color, composition, 16¼ x 10¾".
Collection, The Museum of Modern Art, New York. The Louis E. Stern Collection

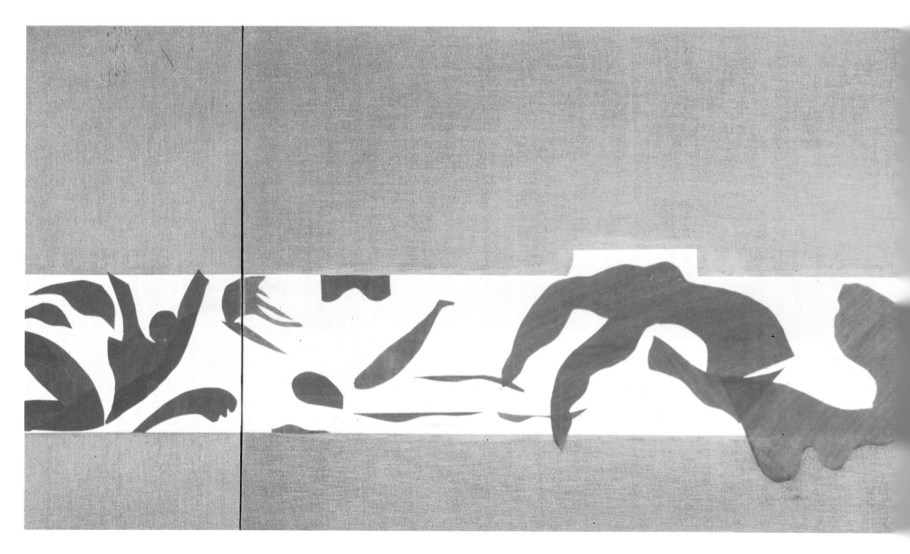

14. *Swimming Pool*. Nice, summer 1952–1953. Gouache on cut-and-pasted paper mounted on burlap.
Nine-panel mural in two parts, 7' 6⅝" x 27' 9½" and 7' 6 ⅝" x 26' ½".

15. *Large Red Interior*. 1948. Oil on canvas, 52 x 38".
Photograph ©Musée National d'Art Moderne, Centre Georges Pompidou, Paris